A WORKBOOK

For

BESSEL van der KOLK's

THE BODY KEEPS THE SCORE: Brain, Mind, and Body in the Healing of Trauma

TABLE OF CONTENTS

How To Use This Workbook

About The Author

Prologue: Facing Trauma

Prologue Analysis

PART ONE | THE REDISCOVERY OF TRAUMA

Chapter 1 Lessons From Vietnam Veterans

Chapter Analysis

Chapter 2 Revolutions In Understanding Mind And Brain

Chapter Analysis

Chapter 3 Looking Into The Brain: The Neuroscience Revolution

Chapter Analysis

PART TWO | THIS IS YOUR BRAIN ON TRAUMA

Chapter 4 Running For Your Life: The Anatomy Of Survival

Chapter Analysis

Chapter 5 Body-Brain Connections

Chapter Analysis

Chapter 6 Losing Your Body, Losing Your Self

Chapter Analysis

PART THREE | THE MINDS OF CHILDREN

Chapter 7 Getting On The Same Wavelength: Attachment And
Attunement

Chapter Analysis

Chapter 8 Trapped In Relationships: The Cost Of Abuse And
Neglect

Chapter Analysis

Chapter 9 What's Love Got To Do With It?

Chapter Analysis

Chapter 10 Developmental Trauma: The Hidden Epidemic

Chapter Analysis

PART FOUR | THE IMPRINT OF TRAUMA

Chapter 11 Uncovering Secrets: The Problem Of Traumatic Memory

Chapter Analysis

Chapter 12 The Unbearable Heaviness Of Remembering

Chapter Analysis

PART FIVE | PATHS OF RECOVERY

Chapter 13 Healing From Trauma: Owning Your Self

Chapter Analysis

Chapter 14 Language: Miracle And Tyranny

Chapter Analysis

Chapter 15 Letting Go Of The Past: Emdr

Chapter Analysis

Chapter 16 Learning To Inhabit Your Body: Yoga

Chapter Analysis

Chapter 17 Putting The Pieces Together: Self-Leadership

Chapter Analysis

Chapter 18 Filling In The Holes: Creating Structures

Chapter Analysis

Chapter 19 Rewiring The Brain: Neurofeedback

Chapter Analysis

Chapter 20 Finding Your Voice: Communal Rhythms And Theater

Chapter Analysis

Epilogue: Choices To Be Made

Epilogue Analysis

HOW TO USE THIS WORKBOOK

As it is with many workbooks, this workbook is developed with the sole aim of providing aid to the readers and prospective readers of Bessel van der Kolk's *The Body Keeps The Score*. The workbook will help those who are new to the subject matter of trauma and the mind gain a fundamental understanding based on the contents of each chapter of Dr van der Kolk's book. The purpose of this workbook is to serve as a companion to the original text; it is meant to help the reader/user better understand the author's perspective on the subject of trauma.

This workbook is a book of practice, and its usefulness can only be quantified by how much knowledge can be gleaned from it as regards to the ideas presented in *The Body Keeps The Score* by Bessel van der Kolk. The user of this workbook is encouraged to put their unique ideas on Dr van der Kolk's thoughts down on paper. By recording their progress and engaging in frequent practices, the user of this workbook will be acquiesced to the lessons from *The Body Keeps The Score*.

This workbook is modelled after the original structure of Bessel van der Kolk's text and spaces have been created to give room for the reader/user's comments on various subject matters and actions that help in the learning process. The workbook has a chapter dedicated to every chapter in Bessel van der Kolk's *The Body Keeps The Score* where the contents of each chapter are summarized and issues related to the themes of each chapter are highlighted. The user can then use the thematic knowledge from these summaries to quickly decipher the author's point of view and draw out unique insights.

A workbook is principally an interactive learning tool, and this workbook encourages the interactive learning process by providing enough space for answers in response to the questions following each chapter analysis. The workbook also includes numerous spaces to take notes at marked checkpoints and a list of actions that can be taken in response to what has been discussed within each chapter in van der Kolk's *The Body Keeps The Score*.

The provision of feedback on the part of the reader/user of this workbook cannot be overemphasized, the function of the workbook is intrinsically tied to the response and activities of its user. The learning process can only be said to have improved —by virtue of the use of this workbook— if the user of the workbook provides the type of feedback that stimulates more discourse based on the contents of the original text. This workbook will have not fulfilled its purpose if its users remain as confused as they were about the subject matter of trauma and the mind after using it. It is the hope of the author that readers demonstrate a cogent understanding of the effects of psychological trauma on the body and mind and this workbook will be a great help in actualizing this hope.

ABOUT THE AUTHOR

Bessel van der Kolk was born in the year 1943 in The Hague, Netherlands. He moved to Hawaii where he studied at the University of Hawaii before he attained his M.D. at the Pritzker School of Medicine in the University of Chicago in 1970 Van der Kolk trained at the Massachusetts Mental Health Centre, Harvard Medical School, specializing in Psychiatry. He completed his medical school residency in 1974 and went on to work as a staff psychiatrist at a clinic in Boston. Doctor van der Kolk also served as a director of Boston State Hospital His work with psychiatric patients encouraged him to focus on researching trauma and post-traumatic stress. Van der Kolk's research work in post-traumatic stress has stretched a couple of decades and he has made significant contributions to the literature of trauma.

Dr van der Kolk is a past president of the International Society for Traumatic Stress Studies and has also served as a fellow or member of numerous associations doing research in trauma. Van der Kolk is currently serving at Boston University's School of Medicine as professor of Psychiatry.

Bessel van der Kolk's publishing history has spanned over three decades with more than 150 peer reviewed scientific papers and books. One of Dr van der Kolk's earliest significant books is *Post-traumatic Stress Disorder* which was published in 1984. He also published *Psychological Trauma* in 1987 and has co-authored other books. He released his widely acclaimed book on the effects of trauma on the mind and body —*The Body Keeps the Score*— in 2014.

Dr van der Kolk has been organizing clinical trials and medical training at the Trauma Centre since it was founded in 1982 while he was practicing at Harvard Medical School as a junior faculty member. Most of the work done at the Trauma Centre focus on the essence of trauma and its impact on the memory of trauma patients. Bessel van der Kolk's work at the Trauma Centre prompted him to lead some of the foremost studies on the psychopharmacological treatments of Post-Traumatic Stress Disorder, he also partook in some of the initial studies on stress induced analgesia. Van der Kolk continued to work on trailblazing research work such as the first neuroimaging studies of Dissociative Identity Disorder and Post-Traumatic Stress Disorder. Bessel van der Kolk also received the first grants to study EMDR and yoga from the National Institutes of

Health. He coined the name 'Developmental Trauma Disorder' to describe what he has found to be a nexus of biological and psychological responses to traumatic experiences which occur over a given period of human development. Van der Kolk has shown specific concern for cases of developmental psychopathology where the effects of trauma are complex due to the developmental stages of patients. Research in developmental psychopathology largely focuses on the nature and effects of trauma in children and younger people. After many years of studying developmental psychopathology, Bessel Van der Kolk supported the establishment of the National Child Traumatic Stress Network in 1999. The National Child Traumatic Stress Network has expanded to about 150 centres that are largely responsible for the treatment of traumatized child patients. These sites of the National Child Traumatic Stress Network also provide support for the families of children who have suffered traumatic stress in the United States. Van der Kolk has supported the use of psychedelic therapies, trauma-sensitive yoga, neurofeedback, and body therapies as treatment for trauma patients.

Bessel van der Kolk has acted as the course director of the annual Boston International Trauma Conference since 1989. The Boston International Trauma Conference invites most of the leading clinicians, scientists, and researchers who specialize in trauma studies, attachment studies, developmental psychopathology,and body-oriented therapies to present new trends and research work in their respective fields each year.

Van der Kolk founded the non-profit Trauma Research Foundation in May 2018 and has given lectures on the effects of trauma in Australia, China, Egypt, Germany, Israel, India, Japan, South Africa, Turkey, Indonesia, India, the Netherlands, New Zealand, the United Kingdom, and the United Arab Emirates.

PROLOGUE: FACING TRAUMA

Trauma is an often denied phenomenon; most people will like to believe that they have no first-hand traumatic experience, neither do they want to see it plaguing their friends and families. However, trauma is not a reality of some faraway land or previous wars, it is alive and well around us. Trauma plagues the average person in seemingly calm environments as it plagues refugees and soldiers from war torn states.

Trauma happens to human beings based on personal experiences such as abuse, psychological neglect, and violent conduct. These unfortunate circumstances are rife in our societies today as some research reports have pointed out. For instance, research in the United States by the Centres for Disease Control and Prevention report that one in five Americans were molested as children one in four people were physically abused by a parent; one in three couples are physically violent toward each other. Many people witnessed physical violence against their mothers or misdemeanours from alcoholic relatives as they matured.

As many people experience violent conduct and abuse, they are quick to ignore the traumatic effects of these incidents and deny suffering any form of trauma at all. Human beings have always had the propensity to recover from unfavourable and unfortunate experiences such as wars and epidemics, but we do not fully heal psychologically at the pace we believe we heal. The disasters we face at various phases in life leave psychological scars behind.

The psychological scars left by traumatic experiences can affect whole communities as they affect individuals and families. Betrayals, unprintable secrets, taboos, and shameful histories shared by a group of people, family members, or friends can also deeply disturb the minds of such persons. This just goes to show how dynamic the nature and form of trauma can be.

Humans can also suffer from trauma indirectly; a friend or loved one who has been directly exposed to traumatic experiences may become cold and unresponsive to those around them leading to a sort of contagious depression and unnecessary transfer of negative emotions.

A violent home or a depressing atmosphere is more likely going to prohibit the expression of joy and positive emotions from persons who live in such circumstances. Patients who suffer from Post-

Traumatic Stress Disorder sometimes have friends and family who suffer bouts of depression and anxiety too.

Trauma really is more common than we think it is, but why is it less spoken about by you and your friends? This is because, fundamentally, traumatic experiences are very unbearable experiences. Those who have been traumatized by an abuse or disastrous incident are always very upset about their experiences and they want to get rid of such memories.Traumatized people want to have peace of mind, and this will be achieved when they cannot remember the terrors they have been through or when they make peace with themselves and their circumstances.

Trauma is more or less the result of a physiological attack which becomes a psychological attack and it becomes very difficult for people to deal with the mixed feelings of shame, vulnerability, anger, and anxiety as they try to move on with their lives. Moving past trauma requires facing trauma head onAs much as the patients of trauma desire to forget their traumatic experience, the brain conversely struggles to discard and deny these experiences with such indelible details. The details of traumatic memory are indelible because they are regrettable and despicable events, the most insignificant hints are usually enough to revive memories of the dangers of which one was exposed tofrom a traumatic experience The brain then acts on impulse to protect the body from the previously shelved traumaticexperience. Some of these impulsive actions are aggressive and incoherent so that the person suffering these effects of posttraumatic stress loses confidence in their ability to control their emotions and bodily reactions.

Bessel van der Kolk's interest in medicine was developedwhen, as a teenager, his cousin described the complex functions of the kidneys. He was intrigued by how the human body workedas he studied medicine and he became more interested in theenigmatic nature of the human mind as he studied psychiatry. It is van der Kolk's belief that since the secret of the healing of the human organism lies in the comprehension ofhow it works, the secret of the healing ofpsychological ailments lies in the comprehension of the mind and how it works. The stumbling block of psychiatry remains the understanding of the mind and the brain at asimilar range as the understanding of other parts of the human organism.

Although there is a dearth of psychological knowledge when compared to physiological knowledge, the development of neuroscience, developmental psychopathology, and interpersonal neurobiology has helped clinicians better understand the nature and scope of trauma, psychobgical abuse, and psychological neglect.

The fields of interpersonal neurobiology, neuroscience, and developmental psychopathology have reported a few facts contributing to the knowledge of the mind and psychiatry one of such crucial facts is that trauma forces a few changes to the brain and affects its psychological response system which is casually known as the alarm system of the brain. There is also proof showing that trauma can increase theactivity of stress hormonesand disrupt the brain's ability to separate irrelevant information from relevant information. This helps us understand why there is a certain level of paranoia and excessively vigilant or defensive behaviour in traumatized persons.

Since it has been discovered that the peculiar behaviors of trauma patients are the direct results of significant changes to some brain functions, it has become possible to deviseprocedures and methods to reverse the traumatic process in traumatized individuals. Such recovery procedures take advantage of neuroplasticity (the brain's natural ability to adapt to new circumstances and conform to new patterns of learning or receiving information) in order to improve the alertness of the traumatized brain, help maintain focus on events at hand, prevent reflexive response of hints of previous traumatic events, and collation of information based on relevance.

The study of traumatic stress and its effects on the body and mind have remained Dr Bessel van der Kolk's life's work; most of his concerns can be summarized to the mapping of the human mind and the use of continuous psychiatric discoveries to heal the minds of patients. Van der Kolk's research and work at the Trauma Centre in developmental psychopathology and trauma has involved traumatized patients who have survived wars, natural disasters, child abuse, rape, accidents, neglect, violence in correctional facilities, and human trafficking.

The Trauma Centre has treated children and adults alike, and there is ongoing research to determine the most effective treatments for specific psychological issues and age groups The Trauma Centre receives grants from the National Institute of Mental Health, the Centres for Disease Control, the National Centre for Complementary and Alternative Medicine, the Centres for Disease Control, and numerous foundations to carry out research and trainings in the various possible types of trauma treatment.

Despite the progress made in the effective utilization of yoga, neurofeedback, EMDR, and medications, the bigger challenge remains the ability of patients to overcome traumatic memories and preventing such paralyzing thoughts from taking over their minds at all.

Communication is key to the mastery of traumatic memories and interpersonal relationships could support the efforts of medications to keep the mind calm without paranoia. There is no singular treatment for traumatized people and it takes a combination of multiple treatment procedures to help patients.

The Body Keeps the Score highlights every treatment method employed by Dr van der Kolk and his colleagues at the Trauma Centre and the result of each treatment is dependent on the psychological history of a patient and the uniqueness of their traumatic experience.

Bessel van der Kolk wrote *The Body Keeps the Score* as a guide and as an invitation to understand trauma. The book invites the readers to face the reality of trauma in our world in order to be well equipped to help traumatized people and prevent the development of trauma and traumatic stress in others.

PROLOGUE ANALYSIS

Van der Kolk's prologue to *The Body Keeps the Score*, titled 'Facing Trauma', is a commanding account of the author's perspective on medical enquiries into trauma. The prologue serves its role as a preamble to the main chapters of the book by giving the reader a short and useful lesson on trauma and its effects Bessel van der Kolk writes from a wealth of experience which includes practicing, teaching, and developing of psychiatry for three decades. The author reports how traumatic stress is shared between those directly suffering from traumatic events and those close to such direct sufferers.

The prologue's primary aim is to provide an introductory piece of information and urge readers to empathize with trauma patients. It quickly identifies some characteristics of traumatic stress in patients and highlights the frequency of traumatic experiences such as child abuse, natural disasters, rape, warfront experience, et cetera. Van der Kolk includes a personal note of how he found his interest in medicine and psychiatry in order to intimate the reader with his vision of psychological healing through an in-depth understanding of the mind. The prologue, according to the author himself, is an invitation to study trauma alongside him. This invitation is Bessel van der Kolk's attempt to capture the reader's attention just as they are about to confront the ideas contained in the chapters of the book.

Facing Trauma concludes with the author's clarification of what the book is about and he urges its readers/users to utilize *The Body Keeps the Score* as a guide into the inquiry of trauma. Ultimately, it is Bessel van der Kolk's wish that this book will inspire more discourse, action, practice, and discoveries on the effects of trauma in human beings.

PART ONE

THE REDISCOVERY OF TRAUMA

CHAPTER 1 Lessons From Vietnam Veterans

The first chapter of *The Body Keeps the Score* begins with a tale from Dr Bessel van der Kolk on his first day working as a psychiatrist at a clinic for war veterans in July 1978. It was on this day that Dr van der Kolk met Tom at the Boston Veterans Administration Clinic Tom, a marine who served during the Vietnamese war, had been suffering from Post-Traumatic Stress Disorder and could not stay calm in his home during boisterous celebrations such as the Fourth of July. He had recently spent the weekend in his office in order to avoid acting violently towards his wife and two kids because of the fireworks and loud noise. His sleep has also been distorted with deathly nightmares from his time in Vietnam. His life seemed empty to him and he was in need of real help.

The veteran's story resonates with Bessel van der Kolk's childhood memories. He grew up in Holland as it recovered from the Second World War. Van der Kolk's father had opposed the Nazis and had been sent to an internment camp. His uncle had also been captured in the Dutch East Indies and enslaved in Burma. Both his father and uncle had episodes of exhibiting violent tempers, they never recovered from their wartime trauma. His mother hardly spoke of her childhood either and was always upset whenever she thought about such days.

Tom also explained that his father, who served in the Second World War, acted with rage and coldness toward him and his siblings too. They had both served in the war front and suffered the backslashes of traumatic memories such as the loss of their comradesAlthough Dr van der Kolk prescribed some newly introducedpsychoactive drugs to deal with Tom's nightmares, Tom refused to use the drugs. The veteran feared thatgetting rid of his nightmares would also lead to the disposal of the memories of his dead comrades.

Numerous veterans, stuck in the trauma of the past, who occasionally flew into uncontrollable ragewere patients of Dr van der Kolk. In his search to help these trauma victims, his search for a book on trauma led Bessel van der Kolk to *The Traumatic Neuroses of War* written by Abram Kardiner and published in 1941. Abram Kardiner's book described the effects of trauma on shell-shocked soldiers, the continued feeling of despair, futility, loss, and solitary existence. Kardiner described these adverse effects of trauma as "traumatic neuroses" and described the root cause of trauma to be physical rather than psychological.

In the absence of any accurate compendium of psychological trauma complications, clinicians like Bessel van der Kolk rely on studying their patients in order to understand how trauma torments people directly or indirectly and how to remedy the effects of trauma.

NOTES

....

....

....

....

....

....

....

....

To figure out a solution for trauma patients, the author believes the traumatic memories of the patient must be identified and revisited. For many Vietnam veterans like Tom, Dr van der Kolk granted a series of doctor-patient interviews in order to know their true war experience. Many of the veterans were well prepared before service and cultivated healthy friendships. Tom's closest friend, Alex, was an Italian from Malden, Massachusetts.

Three months into their stay in Vietnam, Alex alongside many of Tom's comrades were killed in an ambush in a ice paddy. Tom could only watch helplessly as his friend was brutally gunned down until a helicopter came to retrieve the few surviving soldiers. Tom, in a fit of vengeful rage, looted a town the following day, killing innocent persons, children, and raping a woman.

Tom's actions the day after Alex's death were a source of great shame for him that it took him months to recount the events after telling what happened in the rice paddy the day before. Tom could not come to terms with his own atrocities and the memory of the cause and effects of his initial trauma continued to haunt him years after his return from Vietnam. Sarah Haley, a colleague of Bessel van der Kolk, supports this idea in her article "When the Patient Reports Atrocities" where she reports how soldiers continue to suffer from the memory of their actions and inactions during war.

NOTES

....

....

....

....

....

....

....

....

Those who suffer from traumatic experience often find it difficult to express deep emotional feelings to those around them. Tom exhibited this emotional numbness too, he could not convey emotional warmth to his wife and children even though he wanted to

Tom's emotional numbness was affecting him too, he felt little or no emotion in his heart. He was less passionate about anything in particular and the only intense emotion he ever showed was anger or rage. This numbness made Tom feel alien to even himself, he struggled to acknowledge his existence and lacked true purpose. He kept watching his life, profession, and family with the eyes of a foreigner. He felt dead on the inside although he felt alive again in an intense legal battle that reminded him of actual combat.

After dedicating so much time and effort to the case, he succeeded in defending his client in that murder case but he suddenly fell back into a feeling of no purpose. He became overwhelmed with the impulsive rage and nightmares so much that he moved out of his home and tried to make himself busy. He drowned his fears and trauma with alcohol and drugs as he isolated himself in a motel room considering signing up as a mercenary in other ongoing wars.

Tom wanted a thrill so frightening to overcome his numbness and emotional displacement. A dangerous and nearly deadly ride in his car on a highway, for some hours, eventually helped calm him down enough to leave the motel and return home to his family.

NOTES

....

....

....

....

....

....

....

....

Bessel van der Kolk conducted many studies at the Veterans Administration Clinic and one of such studies led him to observe the effects of trauma on perceptions. The story which captures Dr van der Kolk's study on the changes made to imagination and perception due to trauma is that of Bill who served as a medic in the Vietnam War. Bill met the doctor when he enrolled in van der Kolk's nightmare study. Bill had schooled at a theological seminary after the war and was in charge of a parish and its congregation. However, Bill was confronted by his traumatic memories from Vietnam soon enough.

Bill had taken responsibility for his new-born child when the vivid images and sounds of bloodied children occupied his mind whenever his baby cried out Bill sought medical help as he began to panic and he was initially thought to be suffering from paranoid schizophrenia because of the sights and sounds he was perceiving out of the blue.

Bessel van der Kolk took over Bill's treatment, gave him a few medications to calm him, and invited him to his nightmare study where he took a Rorschach test to determine how mental images were formed in Bill's mind and what kind of mental images were preoccupying his mind.

Van der Kolk wanted to confirm the traumatic memories affecting Bill before deciding on the method of treatment to apply. The ink blot Rorschach test made Bill recall in horror a dying child who was blown up and bleeding profusely. It was the second ink blot card that triggered Bill's traumatic flashback to that scene of the dying child he could not save. Bill was panicking as he relived the traumatic events of that day and this helped Dr van der Kolk to realise the seriousness of trauma altered perceptions.

21 more veterans were given the Rorschach test and 16 veterans reacted in horror to the same ink blot card, recounting a traumatic

event and making meaning out of the ink blot. The majority of these veterans described the images of corpses and remains of their comrades in shock while a few claimed to see nothing but the ink.

The ink blot test were meant to invoke random images in the minds of people who saw it but the mind of traumatized war veterans had the tendency to impose a certain traumatic event or image on random motifs and circumstances in their surroundings—in short, their perceptions were often distorted by trauma. The few veterans who saw no image but mere ink had probably lost the ability to imagine images similar to the splash of ink, their minds seemed bereft of the gift of imaginations of any kind.

The absence of mental flexibility was also a problem exhibited by these veterans. Those who saw an image in the ink blot continued to see the same traumatic images from the same traumatic event, while the other veterans saw nothing. These Rorschach tests revealed that traumatized persons perceive and imagine the world around them in noticeably different ways. An ink blot could appear to be a butterfly or leaf to a regular person but a splash of blood or a floating ghoul to a traumatized person. This reorganization of perception obstructs a dynamic and creative mental process in a trauma patient, stalling the joy and tranquillity of such a person.

NOTES

....

....

....

....

....

....

....

....

The number of traumatized war veterans seeking medical help greatly outnumbered the available medical practitioners who were qualified and many of them had to wait. The longer these veterans stayed on a waiting list, the longer they had to suffer traumatic stress. Some of these traumatized veterans continued to be a problem to their families and communities because of their violent tendencies, there was a worrying rise of suicide cases of war veterans too.

Dr Bessel van der Kolk allowed some of the veterans hold group meetings as they waited for a proper psychiatric check-up. A group of younger veterans initially refused to talk about their time in the war but found nothing else to speak on. They later succumbed to their conversations about the war and were more eager than expected to talk about a war that was the source of their trauma.

The group of veterans insisted that Dr van der Kolk became a part of their unit and offered him a birthday gift of a marine captain uniform to mark his initiation to their ranks. Another group of older veterans from World War II also insisted that Dr van der Kolk be considered a fellow and presented him with a military grade wristwatch as a Christmas present These war veterans only felt the necessity to discuss their war experiences with fellow soldiers or people who are acquainted with war trauma.

These veterans (the young marines and old soldiers) talked less to their families because their families did not experience the war with them and they talked less of their families because they were only very interested in, or preoccupied with, their wartime experiences. The veterans only came alive to talk about their trauma.

NOTES

....

....

....

....

....

....

....

....

The earlier attempts to treat the war veterans of their various psychological problemsat the Veterans Administration cliniowere far from accurate and diagnoses were not so reliable either. The books on psychiatriy offered outdated treatment methods which failed to meet the needs of many trauma patients and some drugsendered many trauma patients lethargic. While trying to help traumatized persons, they were mistakenly made to experience flashbacks of their traumatic memories and sent into a state of panic. Many traumatized patients were not getting any better.

In the midst of psychiatrists' confusions, some veterans from the Vietnamese War with psychoanalysts Robert Lifton and Chaim Shatan introduced a proper classification for the psychological challenges of many war veterans to the American Psychiatric Association called Post-Traumatic Stress Disorder in 1980.

The diagnosis of Post-Traumatic Stress Disorder grouped the numerous common symptoms of shell-shocked and traumatized patients, the war veteran finally had a definite name for their psychological problems. With the new diagnosis came a new generation of research and inquiry into the nature of the traumatized patient.

After leaving the Veterans Administration Clinic, Dr van der Kolk started working at the Massachusetts Mental Health Centre of Harvard Teaching Hospital in 1982. He taught psychopharmacology and attended to patients. It was here that Dr van der Kolk discovered that the statistics in the books were grave understatements. Child abuse, neglect, violent relationships, rape and many other traumatic events occurred more often than reported. These patients suffered effects of trauma similar to the war veterans and were traumatized by fellow citizens and family members thus suffering for longer in seemingly safe homes.

NOTES

....

....

....

....

....

....

....

....

The most beneficial objectives of studies of trauma are a reliable understanding of the nature of trauma and awell-defined group of effective approaches to reversing the effects of trauma in affected persons. Over thirty years of working with trauma patients such as

Tom, Dr van der Kolk has come to fully understand many developments of trauma, their effects, and possible trauma remedies.

Several research papers and books on new information in trauma studies have been produced and brain scanning were already possible in the 1990s. The discoveries made possible by these researches and new technologies have helped reveal the direct impact of trauma on the brain.

Traumatic events leave imprints on the mind of the patient, the mind is then plagued with flashbacks and images or sounds of such events inordinately. The perception of the traumatized person is often skewed by the details of their traumatic experience and their imagination is limited or blocked by the overpowering essence of a dreaded traumatic memory.

Trauma directly affects the biological processes of a traumatized person, they remain hypervigilant or paranoid without any reason to be so, and they have panic attacks on the slightest hint of a detail of their traumatic experience. For people to overcome their trauma, they must realize that the experience has truly ended along with its terrors. The traumatized brain must overcome the traumatic

overdrive it has been placed in for months or yearsand become fully
acquainted with the present.

NOTES

....

....

....

....

....

....

....

....

CHAPTER ANALYSIS

LESSONS

1. <u>Trauma is a war reality, it can last a lifetime when left unattended.</u> _____

   _____

2. _____

   _____

   _____

3. _____

   _____

   _____

4. _____

   _____

   _____

5. _____

   _____

   _____

6. _____

   _____

   _____

ISSUES SURROUNDING THE SUBJECT MATTER

1. _____

2. _____

3. _____

4. _____

5. _____

6. _____

ACTIONS

1. _____

2. _____

3. _____

4. _____

5. _____

6. _____

CHAPTER 2 Revolutions In Understanding Mind And Brain

Dr Bessel van der Kolk had experienced a paradigm shift in the medical practice of treating mental challenges when he took a job as an attendant at the Massachusetts Mental Health Centre during a break from medical school. Working with a segment of a research group, van der Kolk organized activities to help keep patients preoccupied with regular tasks on a daily basis.

The aim of the whole research at the mental health centre was to determine the relative effectiveness of the use of drugs or the application of therapy in the treatment of young patients diagnosed with a first diagnosis such as schizophrenia. Dr van der Kolk's team focused on engaging their group of patients with camping trips, group lunch, football games and other social events.

A therapeutic approach known as the *Talking Cure* had been adopted by the MMHC and a compound known as Chlorpromazine —developed in the 1950s— was utilized by the mental health centre as an effective medication for psychiatric patients. The *Talking Cure,* which was a type of psychotherapy developed on some of Sigmund Freud's theories of psychoanalysis, helped patients retrace their steps in traumatic memory while Chlorpromazin, developed by a team of French scientists and branded as Thorazine, helped to relieve patients of their delusions and agitations.

Bessel van der Kolk, still a student attendant, had little responsibility to the patients but he observed the extent of trauma, depression, schizophrenia, and many new psychiatric challenges. The field was still developing and some psychological issues were yet to have treatments, so the doctors could only observe and monitor such patients.

NOTES

....

....

....

....

....

....

....

While Bessel van der Kolk worked as a student attendant at the Massachusetts Mental Health Centre, he also experienced trauma patients having sleepless nights and talking about their traumatic memories through the night. These patients had an urge to reveal some secrets about the abuse or violence they endured some time ago. Many of the doctors missed these confessions and revelations of their patients at midnight so they are often left to guess the genesis of their patients' trauma and despair.

Interns and student attendants like Bessel van der Kolk who had no professional business with the diagnosis of the psychiatric patients could only watch in silence as the doctors tried to manage the traumatic stress of these patients without establishing certain facts about them. The cause of their trauma was rarely linked to abuse, rape, a violent home, or neglect. Genuine interest in the patients' lives was minimal and this often hindered progress in their treatment.

A young Dr van der Kolk also met his trauma patients who were willing to talk to him when he worked at night about some type of abuse and neglect they endured prior to seeking psychiatric help.

Many psychiatric patients were misunderstood greatly and the real conversations on calm nights sometimes revealed what had been formerly misconstrued. The sexually weird reactions of the bodies of trauma patients were consistent with the response to traumatic events of sexual abuse whilesome of the violent conduct of patients paralleled the body's memory of violence and self defense.

NOTES

....

....

....

....

....

....

....

....

Bessel van der Kolk continued his studies after his year as a student attendant and returned to Massachusetts Mental Health Centre to start his medical practice. The mental health centre was a place of innovation and medical discoveries,it was also a place of intense examination of the patients. Dr van der Kolkand his colleagues were urged by their teacher, Elvin Semrad,to focus more on thepeculiar realities of their patients rather than the prescriptive suggestions of textbooks.

A close observation of patients who required psychiatric help —what they loved, who they loved, what they cared for, and what they did not care for— was a crucial part of the attempt to understand and reverse their mental suffering, according to Dr Semrad. The suffering and mental health issues many patients will ever have is a result of denial of a certainly disturbing historical fact.

In the 1970s, after the results of the research in which Dr van der Kolk served as a student attendant, it was reported that medication had a more effective impact on psychiatric patients than therapy. There was an increase in the practice of psychopharmacology and the classification of disorders made Psychiatry more scientific in its approach to suffering. These disorders could then be treated using some tested chemical compounds such as lithium(used to manage depression and suicidal thoughts).

The study of chemicals and hormones in relation to psychological issues led to a paradigm shift in the approach to the patients suffering from trauma or other psychological maladies.

NOTES

....

....

....

....

....

....

....

....

In search for more methods and understanding the nature of trauma, Dr van der Kolk's interest in the emerging neuroscience field grew and he listened to some presentations at regular American College of Neuropsychopharmacology meetings. It was in one of such arrangements by the ACNP, in 1984, that he listened to Steven Maier and Martin Seligman's presentation on "learned helplessness" in animals.

The Maier-Seligman research had subjected a few dogs to electroshock treatments in a cage for a period of time. After weeks of painful electroshock treatments inside the cage, they were released and the same treatment was applied to these dogs. As other dogs naturally reacted by running away and trying to escape this harsh treatment, the dogs which had been subjected to the treatment inside a cage tolerated the painful electroshock treatment on the spot.

Betrayal
Trauma
C PTSD ??

The reaction of those caged dogs and a few other experimented animals suggested to Dr van der Kolk that their subjection to inescapable shock treatments affected them in such a way that they chose to endure the shock they were accustomedo than explore new environments or new yet unknown treatments. Dr Bessel van der Kolk then connects this to his traumatized patients who had sought psychiatric help from the mental health team and ultimately returned to a home or place which was the source of their traumatic experience. If traumatized patients are stuck with a known evil or painful treatment, is it possible to help their mind unlearn the "inescapable shock" in order to be free from their traumatic source?

NOTES

....

....

....

....

....

....

....

....

While working with the war veterans at the Veteran Administration centre, Dr Bessel van der Kolk and his colleagues discovered that their patients of trauma were more animated and enthusiastic whenever they recounted their accidents during the war or some dangerous event which caused an amount of trauma. These veterans and many other patients seeking to find psychiatric aid reported that they felt alive whenever they were angry or violent, dangerous activities made them feel whole again.

Sigmund Freud points at a psychological compulsion to repeat some acts in order to feel well in control of anxieties and worries while a Richard Solomon research in the 1970s at the University of Pennsylvania demonstrates how the human body gets used to stimuli from extreme activities. So, the body learns to adapt to discomfort or thrill by repeating scary and dangerous exercises such as parachute jumping and mountain climbing.

This partly explains why trauma patients are addicted to their traumatic experiences. The pain becomes a form of thrll for many traumatized persons so a man can deem a stable relationship to be boring and opt for turbulent or violent relationships just as many people are used to the scare and thrills they get from horror stories In the absence of the fear or horror or pain or abuse, the world loses its spark and withdrawal symptoms such as anxiety and depression set in.

NOTES

....

....

....

....

....

....

....

....

....

Still attending the American College of Neuropsychopharmacology
meetings in 1985, Dr van der Kolk was exposed to the effects of
serotonin on the amygdala's ability to sense sights and sounds as
threats in a lecture given by Professor Jeffrey Gray. While lower
secretion of serotonin forces the person to be more vigilantand
hyperactive. The hyperactivity and unending vigilance of many

patients, who usually had episodes of sudden outbursts, was thus linked to the lower brain serotonin of Bessel van der Kolk's patients.

Dr van der Kolk wondered if finding a way to boost the amount of the neurotransmitter serotonin in the brain was a possible way to help his patients. After the failure of one new product and L-tryptophan to help increase or mimic the needed serotonin levels, a new drug named Prozac was released on the 8th of February 1988 by Eli Lilly. Fluoxetine, branded as Prozac, went on to become a very effective psychoactive drug. Patients who had initially struggled with depression and traumatic stress felt better than they had felt prior to their use of Prozac.

Eli Lilly, the pharmaceutical company that made Prozac, allowed Dr van der Kolk and his colleagues carry out a study on the effects of Fluoxetine on Post-Traumatic Stress Disorder patients. Although Prozac was proven to help the patients with dealing with trauma better than those who were given a placebo treatment, the war veterans who were studied showed no significant improvement still. Prozac helped to increase serotonin production and made the patients less aggressive or anxious, but the situation of the unresponsive war trauma victims remained a mystery.

NOTES

....

....

....

....

....

....

....

....

The impact of pharmacology on Psychiatry is undeniable, the emergence of drugs such as Prozac and Abilify has helped psychiatrists in their bid to give patients a form of succour and remedy. The effectiveness of psychoactive drugs has given more prestige and attention to the field of Psychiatry as many psychiatric patients can now receive treatments that provide favourable results. Doctors are often delighted to have drugs as a more reliable tool to get their job done rather than relying on the more tedious and often slow therapy treatments.

The rise of medications in the treatment of traumatic stress and other psychological issues has also caused a lot of revenue to flow into the pharmaceutical industry. This has prompted pharmaceutical companies to fund many mental health centres and provide grants for research in Psychiatry. Interest in Psychiatry has since improved and several graduate programs continue to reinforce the significance of psychoactive drugs in the field.

However, Dr Bessel van der Kolk sees some potential dangers in this reliance on psychoactive drugs. Firstly, despite the effectiveness of these drugs in mitigating symptoms of psychological disorders, the drugs gradually take away all of the patient's control over their own disorders. Secondly, the larger population has gained easier access to psychoactive drugs yet depression and psychological disorders remain on the rise. Thirdly, some people—including children in foster care and from poor backgrounds— are given antipsychotic drugs even when they necessarily have no need for them with possible consequences on their physical and mental wellbeing as they grow. Lastly, the reliance on medication has led to a reluctance of the medical community to seek out other ways to remedy psychological disorders.

NOTES

....

....

....

....

Pharmacology has provided measured solutions to psychiatric problems and challenges for decades but there are numerous limitations to what psychoactive drugs and psychiatric medications can do today. Dr Bessel van der Kolk proposes a diverse approach to the treatment of traumatic patients which must include natural or non-drug treatments or therapy.

Dr van der Kolk, in agreement with the brain-disease model believes that certain relationships and communication are crucial to any long lasting healing of psychological disorders. If a trusted community can be created and a safe social space where patients can be encouraged to belong to —given a sense of self— and act independently, traumatic stress can truly be remedied.

NOTES

....

....

....

....

CHAPTER ANALYSIS

LESSONS

1. <u>The efficacy of psychoactive drugs for psychiatric disorders</u>
   <u>remains   limited   and   unreliable.</u>
   _____

2. _____

   _____

   _____

3. _____

   _____

   _____

4. _____

_____

_____

5. _____

_____

_____

6. _____

_____

_____

ISSUES SURROUNDING THE SUBJECT MATTER

1. _____

2. _____

3. _____

4. _____

5. _____

6. _____

ACTIONS

1. _____

2. _____

3. _____

4. _____

5. _____

6. _____

CHAPTER 3 Looking Into The Brain: The Neuroscience Revolution

A few technologies for scanning the brain such as the functional Magnetic Resonance Imaging (fMRI) and Positron Emission Tomography (PET) scanners made it possible for neuroscientists to study brain activity and information processing in real time as early as the 1990s. Brain imaging technology allowed Harvard Medical School to lead the vanguard of new neuroscience research.

Scott Rauch, the first director of the Massachusetts General Hospital Neuro Imaging Laboratory, and Bessel van der Kolk decided to see what goes on in the brains of people who have flashbacks and traumatic memories Eight patients agreed to take part in a test that required them to lie inside a scanner and remember a few scenes from a haunting experience. The physiological reactions of a disturbing memory and a calm memory of these volunteers were monitored by Dr van der Kolk and his research team.

The scanners and monitors recorded sudden increases in the heart rate and oxygen levels of the volunteers at the moment a script of a disturbing flashback was read to them, even though they laid still and calm inside the scanner. After the brain scans were printed, they showed a clear activation of the amygdala which is the part of the limbic area of the brain responsible for the response to stimuli akin to danger and the initiation of the stress response from the body. The brain imaging scans show that the amygdala of traumatized persons responds to stimuli or thoughts similar to their traumatic experience with stress hormones, increasing heart rate, increasing oxygen intake, increased blood pressure, and nerve impulses.

NOTES

....

....

....

....

....

....

The scans from the brain imaging scanners also revealed a significant decrease in activity in Broca's area. Broca's area is a part of the brain that is intrinsically linked to the ability to use words. When brain injury or disease such as a stroke affects Broca's area, the patient will not be able to use words to express themselves. The decrease in the activities of Broca's area of the brain explains the speechlessness traumatized people are subjected to when they are confronted by trauma —war survivors are often staring blankly in silence, traumatized children lose their tongue, and people caught up in violent relationships often choose to stay quiet after struggling to express themselves.

Conversely, the brain scans showed an active Brodmann's area in patients as they went through a script of their traumatic experience Brodmann's area is a part of the brain that is credited with visual information. The traumatized person can recall vivid images from the traumatic memory they have been triggered to remember but they may struggle to put the images to paper.

The psychological effects of trauma can force people to be so confused and lose their ability to articulate words that will describe their trauma in a cohesive manner. They can continue to struggle with present a coherent report of what they have seen or gone through after a long time. However, a flashback can bring the vivid images of traumatic events back to the traumatized person with the same effect as when such events occurred irrespective of the time.

NOTES

....

....

....

....

....

....

....

....

During the scanning of volunteers, it was shown that the right side of the brain was activated and the left side was deactivated as they experienced traumatic flashbacks. From these scans, it was established that both hemispheres of the brain had different roles and a uniquely complementary relationship. While the left hemisphere of the brain is largely concerned with language, analysing, and sequencing, the right hemisphere of the brain is connected to intuition, emotions, and the senses (actual, visual, spatial). So, while the left brain is responsible for expression through words, the right brain is connected —and reacts— to images, sounds, textures and smells of an experience.

Since both hemispheres normally complement each other, the left hemisphere deactivating as the right hemisphere stays activated is problematic for mental health. If one hemisphere of the brain is temporarily switched off, the brain's ability to present perceptions, imaginations, and experience into a coherent report becomes an arduous task. This also hinders the sequential analysis of events to determine cause and effect. With only one side activated, people can lose awareness and control over their mental ability to deal calmly with their anxieties because their bodies cannot differentiate its reaction to a traumatic event and a traumatic memory or flashback

NOTES

....

....

....

....

....

....

....

....

The unique experiences of the volunteers of the physiologicaland brain image scanning became clearer to Dr Bessel van der Kolk as he continued to study the body's response to flashbacks or traumatic memories. As memories of a traumatic event are triggered by a sound or an image, the sudden increase in blood pressure, heart rate, nerve impulses and tense muscles are a result of the stress hormones and adrenaline release.

Adrenaline, known as the flight-fight hormone, is one of the hormones responsible for preparing the body for potentially dangerous situations by influencing the tensions of the muscles, increasing oxygen supply, and raising the heart rate. Whenever people are exposed to a scary or traumatic event their bodies react by producing a number of chemicals including adrenaline which helps prepare them to escape from the dangerous situation or defend themselves.

The problem with traumatized persons is that their bodies release stress hormones and adrenaline whenever they are reminded of their traumatic experience. The adrenaline released in the bodies of trauma patients does not disappear as soon as the traumatizing threat subsides. Normally, the spike in adrenaline release is meant to be maintained for a short period of time but it is maintained in the bodies of trauma patients for longer.

The lengthy increased release of adrenaline in their bodies presents a group of adverse effects considering the fact that traumatized persons suffer flashbacks more often and these flashbacks are as though they are living the same event rather than remembering it.

NOTES

....

....

....

....

....

....

....

CHAPTER ANALYSIS

LESSONS

1. <u>Trauma leaves legible revisions on the function of the brain of an   affected   person.</u>

   _____

2. _____

   _____

   _____

3. _____

   _____

   _____

4. _____

   _____

   _____

5. _____

   _____

   _____

6. _____

   _____

   _____

ISSUES SURROUNDING THE SUBJECT MATTER

1. _____

2. _____

3. _____

4. _____

5. _____

6. _____

ACTIONS

1. _____

2. _____

3. _____

4. _____

5. _____

6. _____

PART TWO

THIS IS YOUR BRAIN ON TRAUMA

CHAPTER 4 Running For Your Life: The Anatomy Of Survival

Bessel van der Kolk was friends with the family of Noam Saul when he witnessed the September 11 attack on the World Trade Center buildings at age 5. He saw a plane crash into one of the buildings from his classroom that morning and was ushered back to his parents along with his other school mates. A day after witnessing that horrible incident, Noam made a drawing of what he saw and showed the drawing to Dr van der Kolk on his visit to the family over a week later. The drawing showed the building on fire after the crash, firefighters trying to quell the blaze, people falling out of the tall building, and a mysterious trampoline on the ground.

The trampoline was an imaginative addition of five-year old Noam who said that he wished to include the trampoline so that those who fall from such a tall building would not get hurt next time. This incident shows that although Noam saw the tragedy of that day, he was able to move past it and imagine alternate outcomes of such a terrible experience. Noam's quick recovery can be credited to a number of factors including his proximity to the event, his lack of immediate loss, and his privilege of being surrounded by love from his family.

Trauma patients, on the other hand, are stuck in the events of their traumatic experience in such a way that it becomes difficult to separate the past traumatic event from their present experience. As a result of this, traumatized persons often do not have the sort of adaptive response to threats or traumatic memory such as Noam's imagination.

NOTES

....

....

....

....

The brain's alarm system is always triggered in the face of danger and this allows a number of nervous and endocrine system reactions such as release of stress hormones to kick in. If this process is truncated, the body's reaction to subsequent similar situations—no matter how subtle—will continue to be influenced by continuous release of stress hormones.

The primary function of the human brain is to ensure survival. The brain registers the most important needs of human beings and formulates plans to meet such needs. The brain is built on layers, from the most primal parts which are responsible for primary functions to the most sophisticated layers which grant idiosyncratic features.

The frontal lobe of the human brain isassociated with the emotions such as empathy. The state of the frontal lobe is thus crucial for interpersonal relations with the expression of compassion and empathy.

The amygdala acts as a smoke detector for the brain, it helps in the processing of possible dangerous situations and relaying of such dangers to other parts of the brain.

While the amygdaladetects and processes danger, the frontal lobes (especially the medial prefrontal cortex) serves as a watchtower. Psychological disorders such as Post-Traumatic Stress Disorder cause rapid shifts between the functioning of the amygdalaand the frontal lobes.

The rational part of the brain and the emotional part of the brain often work in a complementary manner but psychological issues may force them to work independently like a rider and horse in disagreement.

A couple experienced a horrible accident involving over seventy cars and a gruesome death of a lady. Long after they were rescued from their car, they remained stuck in the exact emotional response to the event whenever they were reminded of it. Their individual reactions, however, were different.

The term 'dissociation' refers to the essence of trauma which is often presented in fragments and split images of traumatic memory.

The essence of trauma keeps forcing traumatized people's brains to continue releasing stress hormones

As soon as the 'smoke detector' goes into overdrive, the brain momentarily loses sense of time.

With the momentary pause in time, the thalamus cannot piece the imprints and fragments of traumatic memory together so the memory remains incoherent but affective in its many parts.

When Stan and Ute were scanned , Stan's heart rate increased rapidly, his adrenaline shot up, and his blood pressure went up as he had a flashback. His wife, Ute, was not affected as her husband was. Instead, Ute's brain activities were lowered and her body seemed to slow down as she had her flashback. She was frozen.

It remains crucial for the body to learn to reactivate the timekeeper whenever the traumatic memory is initiated and the traumatized person is taught how to differentiate memories from present events.

NOTES

....

....

....

....

....

....

....

....

....

CHAPTER ANALYSIS

LESSONS

1. <u>A traumatic experience can suspend the brain and its</u> <u>imagination in the same moment of</u> <u>trauma.</u>

2. _____

_____

_____

3. _____

_____

_____

4. _____

_____

_____

5. _____

_____

_____

6. _____

_____

_____

ISSUES SURROUNDING THE SUBJECT MATTER

1. _____

2. _____

3. _____

4. _____

5. _____

6. _____

ACTIONS

1. _____

2. _____

3. _____

4. _____

5. _____

6. _____

CHAPTER 5 Body-Brain Connections

Charles Darwin's *The Expression of the Emotions of Man and Animals* was published in 1872, it was his attempt to study the complex nature and workings of emotions in human beings and mammals. Among the numerous ideas presented by the book are Darwin's summation that humans share similar emotional or psychological wants as their mammalian counterparts and that there exists a psychological brain-body relationship. So, humans and mammals display emotional wants or affections such as love, fear, camaraderie, hate, care et cetera while the brain and body share a bilateral relationship as regards emotional responses to stimuli.

Just as a dog would stand with tense muscles and raised hair when they feel threatened humans can also feel the hair on their neck stand with the other effects of a spike in adrenaline whenever they find themselves in dangerous situations. This suggests that psychological reactions are obviously linked to biological processes and psychological disorders leave physiological marks on the body.

Most of us are well aware of the expression "gut feeling" and how emotional distress can actually cause a great deal of pain in the chest or a nagging discomfort in the gut. According to Darwin's *The*

Expression of the Emotions of Man and Animals, the gut maintains an intimate connection with the heart and the brain through a "pneumogastric nerve" which explains why the psychological effects on the body can cause such intense stress on the body that people sometimes look for ways to ease the stress by reacting violently to objects around them or inflicting a different type of pain on themselves.

The regulatory autonomous nervous system(ANS) is split into the sympathetic nervous system (SNS) —necessary for arousal and emotional reactions via the endocrine system— and the parasympathetic nervous system (PNS) which serves as a none emotional part of the nervous system which halts the actions of the SNS whenever necessary.

The heart rate variability (HRV) is a measurement of the fluctuations which occur between the SNS and the PNS. Hence, the proper functioning of the autonomous nervous system as a whole unit can be determined by checking the heart rate variability.

Human beings are social beings and traumatized people often struggle to socialize or relate with their community, this is because trauma makes the world look unsafe. Trauma patients must find a safe space where they can express themselves and reciprocate their feelings. Sometimes, if it is rather difficult to initiate the process with humans, companion animals such as horses, cats and dogs can help traumatized persons socialize and exchange their feelings with a fellow.

Before trauma shuts anyone down, there are usually two levels of safety before total collapse when challenged with danger. The first level of safety is the social engagement level where one responds by calling out for help. The second level of safety is the fight or flight level where one is tensed up and prepared to defend oneself or escape. While the third level is that of collapse where the body simply freezes and awaits defeat.

The fight or flight level of safety is the body's last resort to imminent danger, it is the body's last means of getting to safety. But collapse is the paralysis which is sometimes ascribed to overwhelming fear; the body simply slows down metabolism and attempts to conserve whatever energy is left.

Trauma patients will benefit more if they are exposed to new treatment methods which focus on an emotional engagement system and aim to train the sympathetic nervous system and the parasympathetic nervous system to function optimally.

NOTES

....

....

....

....

....

....

....

....

CHAPTER ANALYSIS

LESSONS

1. <u>The body-brain connection is a shared psychological trait</u>
   <u>between   humans   and   animals.</u>

   _____

2. _____

   _____

   _____

3. _____

   _____

   _____

4. _____

   _____

   _____

5. _____

   _____

   _____

6. _____

   _____

   _____

ISSUES SURROUNDING THE SUBJECT MATTER

1. _____

2. _____

3. _____

4. _____

5. _____

6. _____

ACTIONS

1. _____

2. _____

3. _____

4. _____

5. _____

6. _____

CHAPTER 6 Losing Your Body, Losing Your Self

The sixth chapter of Bessel van der Kolk's book is concerned with the effects of psychological neglect or trauma on the body and self. One of his patients, Sherry, had grown up suffering from neglect. Her mother was in charge of a foster home where she invariably took in many children and released them shortly after a given period of time, Sherry had also cared for some of these children herself but her mother did not show much care for her. Sherry suffered from neglect and subsequently developed a habit of picking at her own skin until she hurt herself time and again. Psychiatrists could not compel her to stop inflicting wounds on herself and she could not will herself to stop either.

Whenever a person suffers from neglect or trauma, and they are sure that they have no one to turn to for help or comfort, they sometimes begin to experiment with their bodies and foreign substances such as razors, alcohol and drugs. Sufferers of psychological neglect are not necessarily suicidal they want to feel better about themselves via any kind of physiological interaction they can create for themselves.

These patients have a form of dissociation from their bodies and lose their sensory perception often times. So,Sherry knew that she was hurting her body and was aware that it was as a result of the psychological neglect she suffered from but still could not stop the impulse driving her to pick the skin of her arms and chest. Dr van der Kolk suggests that there must also be a focus on the bodies of the trauma and neglect patients to help them overcome their psychological difficulties.

NOTES

....

....

....

....

....

....

It is a very disturbing fact but some trauma patients like Sherry have detached themselves emotionally in such a way that their bodies are not totally theirs. They tend to cut themselves and inflict harm on their bodies as if the body is a foreign entity.Many trauma patients cannot sense themselves and have such numbing experiences that they cannot tell what state a part of their body is in.

We all have an elaborate self-sensing system and this helps us to not only retain our individuality but to also take charge of our body and mind as a connected duo.

When people are exposed to trauma, they sometimes drown out their emotions or try to avoid conflicts of emotions. This constant suppression of emotionsputs the self —that unique identity which distinguishes one from others— under a threat of being eroded gradually. Some trauma patients have reported that they have 'watched themselves' from a distance frequently.

Agency simply refers to the ability of one to take charge of one's life. Self-agency allows one to come to terms with one's emotions and draw a connection between self, mind, and body. Trauma patients are treated with an aim to give them self-agency.

Traumatized people also sometimes do not express themselves emotionally, they simply have no words for how they genuinely feel. It would seem that trauma patients have locked up their ability to articulate words that reveal their fear, anxieties, sorrows, and other emotions.

Traumatized persons need to regain full control of their body before a significant recovery from their trauma can be confirmed. Self-sensing and agency are very important ways to get back up from the paralyzing symptoms of a traumatic event or traumatic memory.

NOTES

....

....

....

....

....

....

....

....

CHAPTER ANALYSIS

LESSONS

1. <u>Psychological neglect often steers people to the process of</u>

   <u>self-harming   and   self-isolation.</u>

   _____

2. _____

   _____

   _____

3. _____

   _____

   _____

4. _____

   _____

   _____

5. _____

   _____

   _____

6. _____

   _____

   _____

ISSUES SURROUNDING THE SUBJECT MATTER

1. _____

2. _____

3. _____

4. _____

5. _____

6. _____

ACTIONS

1. _____

2. _____

3. _____

4. _____

5. _____

6. _____

CHAPTER 7 Getting On The Same Wavelength: Attachment And Attunement

Children and their trauma have a peculiar relationship, and this peculiarity varies from one abused or neglected child to anotherAs Dr van der Kolk worked in the Children's Ward of the Massachusetts Mental Health Centre he saw a wide array of psychiatric challenges in children who have been abused or neglected from whenthey were toddlers till their early teenage years. The effects of trauma and abuse on these children were chronic and heart-breaking. Some of the children compulsively re-enacted the violence and abuse contained in their traumatic experiences while others simply sat frozen and detached from whatwent on around them. Some of these children could not recognize themselves in a mirror and some scowled at every adult who approached them.

Bessel van der Kolk's work with these children involved using Henry Murray's Thematic Apperception Test cards to understand how the minds of these children worked and how to help them feel safe enough to test those around them. The test cards showedimages of everyday life and family activitiesand the children were encouraged to tell a story based on the pictures they were shown. Some of the pictures included a father working in a garage with his children, a pregnant woman deep in thought, and a boy looking down at a broken violin. Children from a neighbourhood school made interpretations with happy endings but most of the children in the Children's Ward of MMHC often made up stories with tragic and violent endings. This sharp distinction between the imaginations of the school kids and the patients in the Children's Ward has prompted Dr van der Kolk to think about the possibility of restructuring the mental maps of traumatized children.

NOTES

....

....

....

....

....

....

....

....

....

'Men without mothers' is a reference to the need for human beings to have someone who will expose them to care and lovein an intimate or familial manner during childhood. Most children suffer a negative psychological impactwhenever their mothers or caregivers are absent at birth and at their most vulnerable times.

The home must serve as a safe haven for babies, toddlers, children, teens, and adolescents. If the home can be truly secure, there are less possible waystrauma can get to the children undetected and unsolved.

Children will have their specific type of parents on a whim of fate, no one gets to decide who their parent will be so they make do with what they have. The parents, caring or not caring,are the human beings they must be attached to in their early years.They will also have to cope painfully with the excesses of such parents if they are abusive or neglectful.

When children cannotlove their parents and cannot flee from them, they are presented with a dilemma:such children remain emotionally conflicted and they cannot seem to stay attached or unattached to their abusive parents as they grow wiser.

The children who have not been able to establish a stable relationship with their abusive and neglectful parents or guardians often suffer long-term problems in their subsequent relationships. A person who spent the majority of their childhood cowering from their parents often live out of sync.

To recover from their lost synchrony, they must fill in gaps caused by a lack of genuine childhood attachments.

NOTES

....

....

....

....

....

....

....

CHAPTER ANALYSIS

LESSONS

1. <u>The deprivation of proper parenthood has majopsychological</u>

    <u>setbacks   in   people.</u>

    _____

2. _____

    _____

    _____

3. _____

    _____

    _____

4. _____

    _____

    _____

5. _____

    _____

    _____

6. _____

    _____

    _____

ISSUES SURROUNDING THE SUBJECT MATTER

1. _____

2. _____

3. _____

4. _____

5. _____

6. _____

ACTIONS

1. _____

2. _____

3. _____

4. _____

5. _____

6. _____

CHAPTER 8 Trapped In Relationships: The Cost Of Abuse And Neglect

When people are abused by those with whom they share a close relationship with, the costs are high and they continue for a very long time. The instance of Marilyn is presented in this chapter. She had a history of abuse which she had shut out of her memory a long time ago. However, the effects of whatever happened to her in the past was affecting her life and relationships with others two decades later.

Marilyn came to seek psychiatric help from Dr van der Kolk after she reacted violently to a close friend (Michael) who had simply brushed his body against hers. Prior to befriending Michael, Marilyn had never felt comfortable or safe around men. She had avoided men until well into her thirties and she only felt safe enough around Michael after a long period of time playing tennis with her. She had invited him to a sleepover at her place and they had slept peacefully until 2 in the morning when Michael turned in his sleep and his body touched hers. She suddenly felt a stranger intruded her privacy and physically attacked Michael who was roused from his sleep in surprise. Marilyn had no clear explanations for her sudden rage and uptight behaviour towards even Michael when she consulted Dr Bessel.

The secret to her fear of men and being ill at ease around them was eventually revealed to be a suppressed memory of sexual abuse as a child.

NOTES

....

....

....

....

....

....

....

....

....

Trauma often leaves the sufferer numb from the dreadful and detestable experience, traumatized personsusually prefer to have their feelings stripped off of them.

Traumatic memory is never coherent, it does not have a begiming, middle, and end. So the memory itself is a broken glass of traumatic images and sounds.

In the process of remembering a traumatic event, one may confront the most unsavoury details of the past such as an abusive home. Many trauma patients grew up hating their homes because they had nowhere else to stay other than with their tormentors. The people who should have cared for them and protected them were in fact the molesters and abusers from whom they could not hide.

NOTES

....

....

....

....

....

....

....

....

CHAPTER ANALYSIS

LESSONS

1. Unpleasant and traumatic memories cannot truly be annulled they continue to exist in our unconscious.

   _____

2. _____

   _____

   _____

3. _____

   _____

   _____

4. _____

   _____

   _____

5. _____

   _____

   _____

6. _____

_____

_____

ISSUES SURROUNDING THE SUBJECT MATTER

1. _____

2. _____

3. _____

4. _____

5. _____

6. _____

ACTIONS

1. _____

2. _____

3. _____

4. _____

5. _____

6. _____

CHAPTER 9 What's Love Got To Do With It?

To know or determine the nature of any given disease is always the primary concern of medical practitioners. Dr Bessel van der Kolk and his colleagues are always challenged by the ability to not only ascribe nomenclature to certain psychiatric conditions of some of their patients but to also determine the sources and possible solutions to such conditions. How are Marilyn's, Tom's, and Martha's psychological needs described and attended to depending on their special needs? These questions were, and remain, the most enduring questions to be asked by a psychiatrist.

The difficulties arising in defining the issues of people who need psychiatric help lie in the peculiarity of the effects of individual traumatic experiences on the brain, mind, and body of the patients. Psychiatry strives to accurately define and determine disorders or diseases with the same accuracy physiological symptoms and diseases are defined but there remains the barrier of the mapping of the mind. The mind-brain-body phenomenon remains largely misunderstood and so healing the mind continues to be an ongoing process with several trials.

The Diagnostic and Statistical Manual of Mental Disorders, since its initial publication, has been a reference point for naming the conditions of many patients and categorizingthe treatment types to be administered to patients but an error margin exists in many diagnoses because the peculiar conditions of such patients are hardly explored for their separate circumstances.

NOTES

....

....

....

....

....

....

....

Recording the origins of some traumatic experiences can be more disturbing and disconcerting than any other process in the treatment of patients. Since traumatic memory is stored as fragments of unpleasant events, it is especially painful for traumatized to go through their traumatic history.

It is known that many traumatized persons struggle to keep themselves in check and, when they cannot control their extreme emotions, they resort to alcoholism, cutting their skin, and experimenting with drugs. Self-harm is usually the traumatized person's way of dealing with intense negative emotions and psychological neglect.

Underlining traumatic stress are the many negative effects tied to it. There is a drug crisis, there are suicidal majorities, there is also the potential to pass trauma from one generation down to another.

The most urgent and widespread problem in the health system is the abuse of children. There are more children abused in their homes than any report of statistics would love to show. So many children are abused and neglected at home with no one else to shelter them, these children are being terrorized under their own roofs and they may helplessly end up viewing the rest of the world as unsafe too.

NOTES

....

....

....

....

....

....

....

....

....

....

CHAPTER ANALYSIS

LESSONS

1. Child abuse, molestation, and neglect are so widespread that

    a   public   trauma   crisis   is   the   result.

    _____

2. _____

_____

_____

3. _____

_____

_____

4. _____

_____

_____

5. _____

_____

_____

6. _____

_____

_____

ISSUES SURROUNDING THE SUBJECT MATTER

1. _____

2. _____

3. _____

4. _____

5. _____

6. _____

ACTIONS

1. _____

2. _____

3. _____

4. _____

5. _____

6. _____

CHAPTER 10 Developmental Trauma: The Hidden Epidemic

The minds of children are very delicate and some earlyemotional scars define certain brain reactions as children mature over the years. There are many groups opposing the idea that children can grow up with certain mental scaring affecting their developmental process. However, it cannot be ignored that many young patients at the mental health centre are experiencing major personal and interpersonal disorders due to developmental trauma. The cases of two-year old Anthony, thirteen-year old Virginia, and fifteen-year old Maria are case studies of developmental trauma.

Anthony, despite his very young age, was brought to see Dr van der Kolk due to his violent tendencies and banging of his head. His mother reported that he acts like that to get her attention and compared him to his absentee father whom she called a good-for-nothing. Maria was obese, violent, depressed, and neglected when Bessel van der Kolk attended to her. She referred to herself as unwanted garbage and she had given up on any positive view of herself. Virginia went through numerous foster homes and was abused more than once sexually and physicaly. She had been sexualized by most persons of the opposite sex she wasacquainted with or in custody of. She described herself as unwanted and wished she was dead.

What all three young patients had in common was neglect and abuse. Anthony's mother obviously neglected him and he was exposed to an unsafe environment, the same can be said for Maria and Virginia in addition to the abuse they suffered. The trauma which they suffer from must be properly analysed and treated based on their personal circumstances rather than "managing" their symptoms and simply labelling them bipolar or schizophrenic.

NOTES

....

....

....

....

....

....

....

....

....

While it might have been speculated before, there are no particularly 'bad genes' responsible for psychological challenges or disorders. Traumatic stress and other disorders are mostly a result of exposure to certain extreme circumstances. However, the strain on the bodies of some sufferers who have been subjected to extended periods of releasing stress hormonescould have some genetic significance in their direct descendants.

The National Child Traumatic Stress Network was established to help many children across the United States gain access to the facilities and services which willsupport their psychological needs as they mature. The work of the NCTSNallows them to collaborate with many schools and provide basic psychological education to the children. Many activities are aimed atencouraging the children to develop trust outside their homes and teaching them how important it is to work actively with their peers. The schools will also have a reorientation of dealing kindly with their pupils.

The family, as the basic unit of the society, goes a long way in determining howchildren and young people develop in a society.A child who grows up with neglectful or abusiveparents will be limited in certain areas of development or maturity, such a child is more likely to withdraw from society and exhibit sociopathic behaviours.

One of the most destructive impacts on interpersonal relationships emanates from an incestuous history of abuse. Most people who have been abused by a family member struggle with this traumatic fact for extremely long periods oftime —usually several decades. Some people will be unable to establish and maintain intimate relationships when they reach adulthood, it is sometimes difficult for them to be intimate with their partners without remembering the breach in trust from that betraying family member.

NOTES

....

....

....

....

....

....

....

....

CHAPTER ANALYSIS

LESSONS

1. <u>Incest has become a common initiation for trauma in a</u> <u>sizeable</u> <u>number</u> <u>of</u> <u>people.</u>_____

2. _____

_____

_____

3. _____

_____

_____

4. _____

_____

_____

5. _____

_____

_____

6. _____

_____

_____

ISSUES SURROUNDING THE SUBJECT MATTER

1. _____

2. _____

3. _____

4. _____

5. _____

6. _____

ACTIONS

1. _____

2. _____

3. _____

4. _____

5. _____

6. _____

PART FOUR

THE IMPRINT OF TRAUMA

CHAPTER 11 Uncovering Secrets: The Problem Of Traumatic Memory

Traumatic memory is the bedrock of the problems traumatic patients keep facing, the unbearable effects of the flashbacks and the severe symptoms that follow can be linked back to a certain traumatic memory. Traumatic memories can bevery delicate pieces of data for psychiatrists in their quest to help psychiatric patients but reaching out to recover these memories is extremely difficult for patients. The intense emotions caused by traumatic memories often cause psychological pain and confusion to those who bear them.

Dr Bessel van der Kolk remembers a patient he examined in 2002 who had reportedly been sexually abused by Paul Shanley as a boy. Shanley had served as a Catholic priest in his parish in Newton, Massachusetts as he grew up. The patient had forgotten about being molested until he was alerted of an investigation of the priest for abusing young boys Dr van der Kolk considered the possibility of the memory being inaccurate and unreliable since it had been repressed for a very long time.

After a comprehensive check and the possible request for the memories as evidence against the priest under investigation, Dr van der Kolk had been exposed to the complexities of traumatic memory as experienced by a traumatized person who initially suppressed it.

NOTES

....

....

....

....

....

....

....

One of the more prominent challenges of traumatic memory is its intensity. Whenever traumatized people are exposed to a hint or stimuli that points at a traumatic event they went through, their mind breaks down under disconcerting and highly uncomfortable sensations as images and sounds from the event appear in bits. The recall of trauma after it has been repressed for so long can be a painful ordeal.

The difference between normal memory and traumatic memory lies in the fact that the details of traumatic memories are more exact and less prone to imaginative additions. Our memories normally come in editions because our perception of these memories have been affected by the course of time and our wealth of experience. However, time hardly distorts the facts of traumatic memories.

Traumatic memories are sometimes repressed and forgotten fo several years. It is a common fact that nobody wants to remember their most horrible experiences, and when some people suffer trauma at an early age they can repress the memory of their traumatic experience and build their life on other memories. Sometimes, the forgetfulness or amnesia is an involuntary effect of the traumatic event itself. The trauma can be so overwhelming on the mind that it cannot reproduce the events in words but the person's body is sometimes compelled to act out its exact reactions at the time of the traumatic experience.

NOTES

....

....

....

....

....

....

....

CHAPTER ANALYSIS

LESSONS

1. <u>The kickbacks of traumatic memory come with unbearable symptoms   sometimes.</u>

   _____

2. _____

   _____

   _____

3. _____

   _____

   _____

4. _____

_____

_____

5. _____

_____

_____

6. _____

_____

_____

ISSUES SURROUNDING THE SUBJECT MATTER

1. _____

2. _____

3. _____

4. _____

5. _____

6. _____

ACTIONS

1. _____

2. _____

3. _____

4. _____

5. _____

6. _____

CHAPTER 12 The Unbearable Heaviness Of Remembering

To speak of the horror of certain traumatic experiences is to live through them again in every detail. The horrors of what war veterans —for example— saw in the world war left many of them so shaken that we can observe the effects on their physical disposition. The dead look in their eyes, their broken physical postures, and morbid facial expressions are enough to reveal the true depth of the effects of their traumatic memories.

The expression "shell shock" had been invented during the First World War and it was as a result of the overwhelming psychological disorders soldiers suffered in the war front of that war. Many soldiers could not cope with the mass wastage of human lives and far-reaching hostilities around the world all at the same time. Nations such as Britain and the United States had initially spent a lot of resources on their psychologically affected soldiers. Britain and Germany would later discourage the diagnosis of "shell shock" or traumatic stress as a condition of war casualties as they prioritized winning the war and boosting the morale of their soldiers more than other things.

However, the weight of traumatic memories continued to rest heavily on society and was recorded in literature. The 1929 novel of Erich Maria Remarque, titled *All Quiet on the Western Front*, captured the state of mind of many soldiers as they remember the war and are stuck in its grotesque memories.

To prove the claims of repressed memory being a scientific reality, a few studies have been conducted. One of such studies shows how a number of ladies who had been abused as children failed to remember that they were ever abused or recalled a completely different case of abuse. While some people remember their traumatic experiences vividly, some people have mentally repressed whatever images they had of their trauma so that they cannot remember the event.

There is a distinction between normal memories and traumatic memories. Normal memories, or memories of normal events, are malleable and subject to several changes over time. The imagination actively reworks our memories Traumatic memories, however, remain untouched by time or imagination. They can only be repressed and concealed but they will stay intact wherever they are stored in the brain.

So many instances can prove how unwanted traumatic memories are and howhumans actively try to get rid of them. Some books on the holocaust and the events in the concentration camps created by the Nazis show how much survivors refuse to see the world with the same eyes that saw the holocaust. The cruelty is often said to be so profound that only those who experiencedsuch cruelty could fathom it —yet, they could not speak of it to others who did not go through the experience.

NOTES

....

....

....

....

....

....

....

CHAPTER ANALYSIS

LESSONS

1. <u>Traumatic memory is a paradox, most people want to be rid of it but it bears down on them every day.</u>

   _____

2. _____

   _____

   _____

3. _____

   _____

   _____

4. _____

   _____

   _____

5. _____

   _____

   _____

6. _____

   _____

   _____

ISSUES SURROUNDING THE SUBJECT MATTER

1. _____

2. _____

3. _____

4. _____

5. _____

6. _____

ACTIONS

1. _____

2. _____

3. _____

4. _____

5. _____

6. _____

PART FIVE

PATHS OF RECOVERY

CHAPTER 13 Healing From Trauma: Owning Your Self

People who have suffered from traumatic stress cannot be cured or necessarily freed from the events that cause them such trauma, neither can the memory of such events be redacted. The aim of Psychiatry is to relieve sufferers of Post-Traumatic stress and other psychological challenges of the life-impacting symptoms of these disorders. Psychiatry does not strive to deny the fact that these unfortunate and disturbing events have taken place, instead it strives to help people recover from the paralyzing clutches of the memories of such events.

People who have PTSD and many other psychological disorders struggle to lead normal lives because of the trauma they keep going through. So, they are often not in control of their present experience as any form of stimulus will initiate flashbacks, a lack of focus, bouts of aggressive reactions, hysterical behaviour, paranoia, paralysis, among a host of other negative effects. The inability to remain calm and in control of all senses due to the slightest hint of threat is the bane of patients who find themselves in the psychiatric ward.

What Dr Bessel van der Kolk stresses in this chapter is the imprint or mark of trauma on his patients and the primary aim of Psychiatry to remove them. The treatment offered to these patients will help them to stay calm whenever they are exposed to images or sounds which resemble their past and integrate with friends and family without fear dictating their every move.

NOTES

....

....

....

....

....

....

CHAPTER ANALYSIS

LESSONS

1. <u>True recovery from trauma is a matter of self-agency rather than regular consumption of drugs</u>.

   _____

2. _____

_____

_____

3. _____

_____

_____

4. _____

_____

_____

5. _____

_____

_____

6. _____

_____

_____

ISSUES SURROUNDING THE SUBJECT MATTER

1. _____

2. _____

3. _____

4. _____

5. _____

6. _____

ACTIONS

1. _____

2. _____

3. _____

4. _____

5. _____

6. _____

CHAPTER 14 Language: Miracle And Tyranny

After a major traumatic experience such as the terrorist attack on the 11th of September 2001, the survivors often require a comprehensive psychiatric check-up. For the city of New York, the authorities suggested Psychoanalytically Oriented Therapy and Cognitive Behavioural Therapy to be used as treatment approaches for New Yorkers seeking medical psychological or psychiatric aid in hospitals. The hospitals could have tried other approaches to help patients but they considered the usefulness of their practical treatments for academic research and the time/cost efficiency of these treatments.

Nevertheless, New Yorkers refused to go to these hospitals to seek professional psychiatric help. The general hospitals recorded low numbers of patients seeking to find psychiatric help in relation to the September 11 attacks. Dr Bessel van der Kolk and his colleagues decided to find out why people refused to use the hospitals and where else they turned to for treatment.

There were indeed patients who wanted to be relieved of the memories and terror of that day but most of them turned to physical therapy, yoga, EMDR, acupuncture, and full body massages to help their bodies and minds to relax. These people were apparently uninterested in the Psychoanalytically Oriented Therapy and Cognitive Behavioural Therapy sessions because they did not want to talk about their trauma. This prompted Dr van der Kolk to question the patient's evasion of talking about their trauma and if there are merits or demerits of not speaking of traumatic events.

NOTES

....

....

....

....

....

....

....

....

CHAPTER ANALYSIS

LESSONS

1. <u>Some trauma patients can convalesce without speaking to a</u> <u>therapist</u> <u>about</u> <u>their</u> <u>memories.</u>

   _____

2. _____

   _____

   _____

3. _____

   _____

   _____

4. _____

   _____

   _____

5. _____

   _____

   _____

6. _____

   _____

   _____

ISSUES SURROUNDING THE SUBJECT MATTER

1. _____

2. _____

3. _____

4. _____

5. _____

6. _____

ACTIONS

1. _____

2. _____

3. _____

4. _____

5. _____

6. _____

CHAPTER 15 Letting Go Of The Past: EMDR

Chapter 15 begins with a patient's case of rage and resentment, and how Eye Movement Desensitization and Reprocessing (EMDR) helped him move past his unpleasant experience. Just like the many people who approached Dr Bessel van der Kolk for professional medical help, David was struggling with a lot of psychological issues at home and at work. He suffered multiple episodes of anger, depression, resentment, and rage. David reported that he had always been unnecessarily critical of his child, rebuking him for every error or mistake made. He also felt cold and less compassionate towards his wife. David was afraid that he was failing to love his family and he was becoming more irritable or less tolerant at work.

David's session with Dr van der Kolk revealed a painful and unfortunate event that happened to him when he was a young adult several years ago; a group of boys had attacked him and slashed one of his eyes with a broken bottle while doing his job. Bitter about the incident and struggling with the fact that he lost an eye, David had become quite vengeful and filled with unbridled rage. He had initially sought out his assailants to deal violently with them but stopped as soon as he could suppress his malevolent intent.

However, David continued to suffer from the memory of his eye getting stabbed —his trauma mixed up with all its negative emotions affected his interpersonal relationships so much that he was afraid of his own vengeful behaviour. His EMDR session with Dr Bessel van der Kolk helped him to take control of his rage and realize that he was not such a monster. The Eye Movement Desensitization and Reprocessing treatment helped David focus less on his traumatic stabbing memory and get in touch with his compassionate personality.

NOTES

....

....

....

....

....

....

....

....

CHAPTER ANALYSIS

LESSONS

1. <u>Recuperation from rage can be achieved by acknowledging</u>

   <u>one's</u>   compassionate   memories.

   _____

2. _____

   _____

   _____

3. _____

   _____

   _____

4. _____

   _____

   _____

5. _____

   _____

   _____

6. _____

   _____

   _____

ISSUES SURROUNDING THE SUBJECT MATTER

1. _____

2. _____

3. _____

4. _____

5. _____

6. _____

ACTIONS

1. _____

2. _____

3. _____

4. _____

5. _____

6. _____

CHAPTER 16 Learning To Inhabit Your Body: Yoga

Sometimes, the physiological knee-jerk reactions and consequences of trauma in patients must be attended to immediately if there is any hope to address theother psychological issues they have. Dr van der Kolk recalls the case of his patient, Annie. Annie had serious anxiety issues and she could not even look him in the face when they met for the first time. Her legs kept shaking and her head was bowed towards the floor whether she was sitting or standing. Bessel van der Kolk had made her feel at ease by encouraging heto take deep breaths and calming herlimbs. The first therapy sessiononly took this qigong method of breathing betweenthe doctor and Annie then she was given subsequent appointments.

Annie had endured abuse from both her parents as a child and these episodes of brutality had severe effects on her body and mind.She worked helping children with special needs and she was very good at was she did. Annie was responsive when asked about her relationship with the children she worked with butwas unwilling to discuss her relationship with adults. She was married yet she did not speak much about her husband.Annie struggled to be at ease with adults like herself, she found it hard to handle conflict, and she sometimes resorted to self-harm by cutting her flesh with razors.

Her anxiety often made her frozen and unresponsive. In order to calm her physiological symptoms Dr van der Kolk employed a specific breathing technique to stimulate her parasympathetic nervous system and the Emotional Freedom Technique which uses the acupressure points to make her more tolerant.

Yoga reveals a lot in trauma patients and people with specific psychological difficulties. For instance, a traumatized person might be dissociated from their self and remain so until they are challenged to use their bodies as an extension of their self. Yoga often increases the sense of responsibility and self-agency in PTSD patients, Annie came to relate more with herself and perceive her body as a less foreign or separate entity.

NOTES

....

....

....

....

....

....

....

CHAPTER ANALYSIS

LESSONS

1. <u>Trauma-related tensions and anxieties can bestopped by the</u>
   <u>habits</u>   <u>of</u>   <u>self-</u>
   <u>awareness.</u>_____

2. _____

   _____

   _____

3. _____

   _____

   _____

4. _____

   _____

   _____

5. _____

   _____

   _____

6. _____

   _____

   _____

ISSUES SURROUNDING THE SUBJECT MATTER

1. _____

2. _____

3. _____

4. _____

5. _____

6. _____

ACTIONS

1. _____

2. _____

3. _____

4. _____

5. _____

6. _____

CHAPTER 17 Putting The Pieces Together: Self-Leadership

A rather interesting and confusing psychological condition affected one of Dr Bessel van der Kolk's patients early in his career. Her name was Mary and she was a really shy and lonely young person. She had attended a few therapy sessions with the doctor when, all of a sudden, she started appearing at her sessions assuming other names and personalities. She was at one time a hurt little girl, she was also a flirty young woman, and a raging adolescent. While assuming these other personalities Mary referred to 'Mary' as a different person.

Mary's Dissociative Identity Disorder (DID) was the first DID case Dr van der Kolk dealt with. It was formerly known as Multiple Personality Disorder and the so-called disorder had something to do with fragments of the patient's mind and memories. The disorder made Mary's mind create separate and concrete identities. Although many healthy minds have the capacity, and are fond, of creating personalities and having mental interactions with these creations, it can become a very extreme condition in persons suffering from traumatic stress.

These mental personalities usually represent impulses and certain identities locked within memories. After several psychological treatments and therapies, it has been seen that interacting with these distinct parts of the mind is crucial to the healing of such patients. Unless the patient is acquainted and becomes a master of self, they will continue to exhibit these dissociated identities without control.

NOTES

....

....

....

....

....

....

....

CHAPTER ANALYSIS

LESSONS

1. The mind has the ability to conjure fully developed and
   separate personalities or identities.

   _____

2. _____

   _____

   _____

3. _____

   _____

   _____

4. _____

   _____

   _____

5. _____

   _____

   _____

6. _____

   _____

   _____

ISSUES SURROUNDING THE SUBJECT MATTER

1. _____

2. _____

3. _____

4. _____

5. _____

6. _____

ACTIONS

1. _____

2. _____

3. _____

4. _____

5. _____

6. _____

CHAPTER 18 Filling In The Holes: Creating Structures

People with traumatizing memories, a history of abuse and psychological neglect are usually deprived of certain mental imprints such as parental love, attention, sympathy, approval, et cetera. The psychological neglect such people suffer from often stunts their feelings of self-agency or self-esteem. This is why no matter how much psychotherapeutic help they get, there is still an inadequacy felt as a result of the mental 'holes' and gaps. Parents and families of these patients deprived them of any early impression of compassion, love, acceptance, sympathy, and community. The lack of foundational care, love, or acceptance makes it extremely difficult for trauma patients to fully recover because there are no memories of love and acceptance to refer to as they strive to find acceptance and community.

Dr Bessel van der Kolk met Albert Pesso at a 1994 conference and Pesso had informed van der Kolk that he had discovered a way to help people fully recover from neglect and mental holes through the Pesso Boyden System Psychomotor therapy. This PBSP therapy helps a patient (protagonist) to confront their history of psychological neglect, provides a comforter (contact person) in place of the absentee parents or loved ones, and creates 'structures' to help the patient/protagonist fill up the gaps or holes caused by the psychological neglect they suffered in the past.

The Pesso Boyden System Psychomotor therapy also revealed personal information about Dr van der Kolk's parents influence on his mind some time later. Overcoming his skepticism, Dr Bessel van der Kolk decided to learn about the PBSP therapy from Albert Pesso for its utility.

NOTES

....

....

....

....

....

....

....

....

CHAPTER ANALYSIS

LESSONS

1. <u>Psychological neglect creates mental holes or lacunas which prevents certain persons from being fully capable of feeling loved or accepted.</u>

2. _____

_____

_____

3. _____

_____

_____

4. _____

_____

_____

5. _____

_____

_____

6. _____

_____

_____

ISSUES SURROUNDING THE SUBJECT MATTER

1. _____

2. _____

3. _____

4. _____

5. _____

6. _____

ACTIONS

1. _____

2. _____

3. _____

4. _____

5. _____

6. _____

CHAPTER 19 Rewiring The Brain: Neurofeedback

Dr Bessel van der Kolk's first practical exposure to the brain wave or electroencephalogram was during his part time job at a Boston State Hospital sleep laboratory while he was still in medical school. Van der Kolk was tasked with preparing volunteers at night and recording their brain activity using a pdygraph machine as they slept. While these persons slept, their brains still showed a significant amount of activity as brain waves continued to travel across the neural pathways spontaneously. Sleep cycles were recorded and the electroencephalogram of volunteers were taken while they dreamed.

The ability to record brain waves brought about a lot of progress in the study of the brain and mind. For instance, the recording of electroencephalogram has made it possible to map outcertain 'electric circuits' through which the brain waves move within the brain. The focus on neurofeedback has led to several important research on brain waves, trauma, learning difficulties, psychomotor challenges, and new psychiatric insights.

In 1924, at a time when the medical community was preoccupied with the chemical reactions in the brain, Hans Berger discovered that there were several electrical activities in the brain and this became a major shift in the approach to understanding the brain.Hans Berger, the German psychiatrist, also reported that different brain waves indicated different brain activities. So, the brain waves recorded while speaking will be significantly different from the brain waves recorded while sleeping.

The focus on the study of electroencephalogram has made it possible to map electric circuits or pathways in the brain andimprove knowledge of how the brain functions. In short, the brain of a traumatic stress patient can be studied and brain activities peculiar to them can be determined more easily.This is particularly helpful in people who react to trauma in subtle wayssuch as appearing calm yet seeing vivid pieces of images as the amygdala and thalamus churn on as if the traumatic event is happening all over again.

NOTES

....

....

....

....

....

....

....

....

CHAPTER ANALYSIS

LESSONS

1. The transmission of brain waves are pertinent to the study of
how the brain is formed and how it
functions._____

2. _____

_____

_____

3. _____

_____

_____

4. _____

_____

_____

5. _____

_____

_____

6. _____

_____

_____

ISSUES SURROUNDING THE SUBJECT MATTER

1. _____

2. _____

3. _____

4. _____

5. _____

6. _____

ACTIONS

1. _____

2. _____

3. _____

4. _____

5. _____

6. _____

CHAPTER 20 Finding Your Voice: Communal Rhythms And Theater

The final chapter of Bessel van der Kolk's *The Body Keeps the Score* explores the positive effects of communal relationships and theatre on people who have a psychological challenge. The author, just like many of his colleagues, was inspired to consider theater as a possible treatment method for patients when his son suffered from a so-called fatigue syndrome as a little boy.

He had several bouts of allergic attacks and spells of lethargy so that he could barely go to school. Dr van der Kolk and his wife took their child to evening classes and theatre classes which he could attend in the evenings he had enough strength to move around. He enjoyed role playing and playing important characters helped his recovery very much. He was able to see himself in new characters other than the identity of the hypersensitive child whose ability to learn was restricted. Being able to be part of a learning community their son regained his confidence and sense of competence.

For people to feel in control of themselves, there must be a conscious engagement with daily actions such as walking, sitting, talking, dancing, running, breathing etc. This way, people can freely interact with the rhythm of life with their bodies. Acting makes use of the body, the voice, and the brain. Rather than being stuck in a depressing situation or passive psychological jail people are encouraged to take charge of their lives using their bodies.

NOTES

....

....

....

....

....

....

....

....

CHAPTER ANALYSIS

LESSONS

1. <u>Keeping the body active will help augment the brain's functions and strengthen the mind in cases of mental fatigue or challenges.</u> _____

2. _____

_____

_____

3. _____

_____

_____

4. _____

_____

_____

5. _____

_____

_____

6. _____

_____

_____

ISSUES SURROUNDING THE SUBJECT MATTER

1. _____

2. _____

3. _____

4. _____

5. _____

6. _____

ACTIONS

1. _____

2. _____

3. _____

4. _____

5. _____

6. _____

EPILOGUE: Choices To Be Made

Having read through *The Body Keeps the Score,* it is to be understood that the world is fast becoming a trauma-conscious place. New findings continue to emerge in psychiatric and neuroscientific research today. The continuous study of trauma and psychological disorders in children has also proved to be economically and socially beneficial. Clinicians are now more educated about the brain and the mind than they ever have been in decades. The knowledge gained so far has allowed scientists to present timely interventions which have helped patients improve their level of self-perception, attention, and self-control.

With many years of practice and studies, Dr van der Kolk and his colleagues have innovated several trauma treatment procedures and they better understand how to prevent traumatic stress or other psychological maladies. Many people faced the trauma of abuse and neglect when they were children, at their most vulnerable state. As they grow up with the memories of these traumatic events, the symptoms of psychological stress and internal conflict continue to plague them until they learn how to break out of the chains of such memories. Their behaviours will not change neither will they ever be able to control their emotions if they distrust every person or entity around them. The fear and rage traumatized people feel must be mitigated if they are to become confident enough to challenge their trauma.

The title of the book *The Body Keeps the Score* refers to the psychological assessment of trauma being recorded in the body of traumatized persons as a painful sensation in the heart or gut. The physiological consequences of trauma and traumatic stress have made it clear thatpsychiatric issues will not originate and end up all in the head, the mind and body are fully involved. It is then very important toreach out to traumatizedpeople and help them tovacate the fight-or-flight state they have been stuck in, then their hypervigilance and paranoia must be remedied with a new yet trusted community.

The origin of trauma is mostly rooted in unfortunate relationships such as abusive families, violent friendships, or unsafe neighbourhoods. These aspects of a harmful community leads traumatized people to view the world differently and consider a potential danger in every new person or environment This perception has to be fixed but the traumatized person has to be exposed to a safe space or reinvested in trust in order to help them.

Knowing that trauma comes to affect many people from early childhood, it is in the society's best interest to pay attention to the special needs of younger people. Children are especially exposed to abuse, violence, and neglect because of their vulnerability and relative weakness compared to adults. Adults who are vulnerable usually suffered right from childhood. So, the focus on families and provision of special social support for the children is vital. Governments should not have second thoughts on helping children to stay safe and have access to facilities that will keep them safe. Quality preschool facilities, medical care, and counseling services should be essential for every child in a country.

Helping children to recover from, and open up about, abuse and psychological neglect will make a great difference on a national level. The work done by Dr van der Kolk and his colleagues at the National Child Traumatic Stress Network (NCTSN), since its establishment in 2001, has laid emphasis on children and adolescents. The NCTSN which has more than 150 centers in the United States currently runs a cluster of services including juvenile justice systems, homeless shelters, school programs, residential homes for children and young people, child welfare agencies, and military facilities.

With the help of these services, the National Child Traumatic Stress Network provides good education and information facilities for young people who encounter trauma. Many schools have children who struggle with the traumatic stress of their family members and this gradually becomes their own trauma too. Those who face traumatic events often stay silent and isolated but it is the aim of the NCTSN to help them open up and resolve such developing issues. The children can then recognize themselves, understand that they are wanted and that they are seen, and work towards managing their emotional turmoil.

The NCTSN is trying to make schools a trusted and safe place for children, especially children whose homes might be very unsafe and abusive. The children learn to understand how their bodies and minds work and they learn to be articulate about their experiences. Some of the children who struggle with psychological neglect and abuse cannot communicate effectively because they have been ignored at home for so long. They will then come to school and remain quiet except an intervention such as the activities of the

NCTSN and their school encourages them to utilize language. Teachers are also taught to use language compassionately and considerately when dealing with children who display sudden rage and frustration.

These children and younger persons can improve their self-regulation when they are encouraged to be active in their work at school. They need to get involved at all times, collaborate with their peers, concentrate on their given tasks, and find great pleasure in what they do. Extracurricular activities such as theatre, sports, and games will also improve the child's trust in the safety of the school or a new environment.

Trauma must be dealt with in a more original and reliable way, drugs do not necessarily provide a better solution to psychological disorders. In fact, the overwhelming reliance on drugs to treat psychological disorders has led to numerous disasters. More people use more drugs such as antidepressants and antipsychotic pills than they really need to, people have begun to lose control of their lives. More people die of drug overdose today and alarmingly so, these drugs are usually antidepressants and barbiturates. The generalized ascribing of psychological disorders to people and the immediate recommendations of antidepressants and antipsychotic pills are causing a drug abuse epidemic in the world today.

Trauma and other psychological disorders do not only cause a breakdown of bodily functions but they also challenge the strength and resilience of the human mind. This implies that everyone has the tendency to survive psychological trauma and neglect, the brain is highly adaptable and the strength of the mind is dependent on communal affection.

Likewise, the knowledge of trauma in the society will always pave the way to significant growth out of distress and depression. The urgency of the public traumatic and psychological issues must inspire us to seek out innovative solutions which will help us to achieve a safer community and trusting individuals.

EPILOGUE ANALYSIS

Bessel van der Kolk's fitting epilogue to *The Body Keeps the Score*, titled 'Choices To Be Made', is a short essay which includes the author's current thoughts of the world and the place of trauma in it today. The epilogue serves the role of a final argument to the main chapters of the book by giving the reader a rather compact summary of the lessons on trauma obtained from the pages of *The Body Keeps the Score*. Bessel van der Kolk does not only summarize the main points of this book but he also reveals his hope for a trauma-conscious world with the many advancements in the teaching and practice of psychiatry so far. The author believes that a world with less traumatic stress will gain more economic stability and an increase in the quality of life.

The primary aim of this epilogue appears to be a report of how much progress is being made in the treatment and prevention of trauma in children and the society at large. We are shown that the majority of traumatic stress patients may have had a traumatic memory from childhood. There are so many cases of abuse and neglect against children in their homes and this had led many experts to focus more on the psychological wellbeing of children. Bessel van der Kolk makes an attempt to direct the reader's attention to the facts on trauma in children in order to realize how crucial the work the National Child Traumatic Stress Network does to achieving a trauma free society.